In the beginning, a duck is an egg.

A drawing is a blank page.

A sculpture is a lump of clay.

For my editor, Ann Kelley, who helps words
make their way. Thank you.

—A.B.K.

For my dad, who is always making and
creating—and inspiring me to do the same

—C.K.

Text copyright © 2023 by Angela Burke Kunkel
Jacket art and interior illustrations copyright © 2023 by Claire Keane

All rights reserved. Published in the United States by Random House Studio,
an imprint of Random House Children's Books, a division of Penguin Random House LLC, New York.

Random House Studio and the colophon are registered trademarks of Penguin Random House LLC.

Visit us on the Web! rhcbooks.com

Educators and librarians, for a variety of teaching tools, visit us at
RHTeachersLibrarians.com

Library of Congress Cataloging-in-Publication Data is available upon request.
ISBN 978-0-593-37335-4 (trade) — ISBN 978-0-593-37336-1 (library binding) — ISBN 978-0-593-37337-8 (ebook)

The artist used Procreate on an iPad to create the illustrations for this book.
The text of this book is set in 14-point Cotford Text.
Interior design by Monique Razzouk

MANUFACTURED IN CHINA
10 9 8 7 6 5 4 3 2 1
First Edition

MAKE WAY

The Story of Robert McCloskey, Nancy Schön, and Some Very Famous Ducklings

Written by
Angela Burke Kunkel

Illustrated by
Claire Keane

RANDOM HOUSE STUDIO · NEW YORK

In the beginning, a boy named Bob lives in a place called Hamilton. He wanders the Ohio town with his dog, playing a harmonica, notes trailing behind them.

Bob's mind whirs like a motor and his hands move constantly. Lights flash, buzzers buzz, fuses blow, sparks fly. He makes carvings, large and small. Bob can look at a blank rectangle of soap or the trunk of a tree and see what must be taken away to reveal the shape of a thing.

Years later and hundreds of miles away, a girl named Nancy lives in a place called Newton, just outside the city of Boston. She roller-skates through the halls of her house, her nanny trailing behind her.

Nancy works in her father's greenhouse in the spring. Little hands have little fingers, and she helps with the planting, tamping and watering the soil so that each seed can sprout.

In winter, she winds wire and boughs into wreaths, fingers frozen with cold, sticky with sap. She learns to look—and think—in three dimensions.

But what about the duck, you ask?
Well, it takes twenty-eight days for an egg to become a duckling. It will take Bob and Nancy much longer to become artists.

After Bob finishes school in Hamilton, he wins a scholarship to study art in Boston. His mind is full of *serious* things, *serious* art—Greek gods and Pegasus, Spanish galleons, Chinese dragons—and he tries to draw and paint and carve them. His work is dark and heavy.

But every day on the way to art school, he cuts through the Public Garden and smiles at the ducks.

Many days after school, Nancy goes to the library. She is drawn to big, heavy books with pictures of famous statues. She studies the sculptors' names and their marble carvings, so real they leap off the page.

But these sculptures are in the halls of museums and places far away. Nancy never leaves her town, not yet. She doesn't explore a single gallery, or even the Public Garden. Boston seems like it is at the edge of the world—not her back door.

It is the Great Depression. Bob, worried about how to make a living, goes to visit an editor who makes children's books in New York City.

He gets lost on the streets.
He gets caught in a rainstorm.

And finally, sitting on the edge of a chair in an office, wet as a duck, Bob watches as the editor flips through his gods and galleons and dragons—and then she tells him not to be so serious, and asks him about his hometown instead.

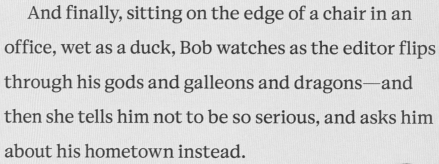

So Bob goes back to Hamilton. He walks the same streets he wandered with his dog and his harmonica. But he also thinks about Boston, about the soft willows touching the pond and how he sat and fed the ducks in the springtime.

What is a wing, a beak, a foot? And how do you know?

Bob knows, because once he leaves Hamilton and lands in New York City, he visits the Museum of Natural History and studies the ducks behind glass.

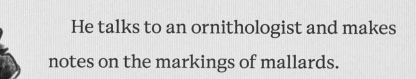

He talks to an ornithologist and makes notes on the markings of mallards.

Finally, he walks to Washington Square Market, and carries home a crate full of . . .

ducks!

They swim in his bathtub.

He lies on the floor while his roommate holds one above his head, so he can see what they look like flying.

And he has to have lots of tissue, because ducks are messy. They use bathtubs, but they do not use toilets.

Bob draws from a duck's-eye view, and a child's view, too.

He shows the fields of Massachusetts, and rivers, and islands, and the feeling of flying above, but also of running your hand along an iron fence while your feet skip down the sidewalk of a city you know well.

Bob works until he has it just right. And finally, in sepia tones, what he captures most of all is a feeling—of looking for safety, of family, and of coming home, all wrapped up in a book.

Yet the worries of World War II lurk
around every corner, affecting everyone,
even a girl like Nancy. When she walks home
from school, boys throw things at her and
call her ugly names because she is Jewish.
Nancy fights back and runs hard.

Still, even into high school, what Nancy can't outrun is the question in the back of her mind—where does she belong? She feels like a seed in the dirt, dormant and waiting to sprout. The only place she thrives is art class, her hands in the clay.

While Nancy works at becoming an artist, she also marries and becomes a mother. Her family grows; they move from state to state.

No matter where they are, Nancy makes space—a dimly lit basement, the corner of an already-cramped bedroom—to shape and mold and carve. When there are small spaces, she makes small things. But she longs for bigger spaces, to do bigger things.

It's hard to do big things when the answer is often *no*. Nancy applies to art shows. One hundred fifty-six rejections come back. With each rejection slip, Nancy is discouraged, but she *never* stops working.

At last, Nancy's family returns to Boston, where she finally has a space of her own.

Soon after Nancy begins work in her studio, a family she knows strolls through the Public Garden for the first time. They have just moved to Boston from another country—but the mother has read Bob's book over and over again, and so, even though they have never been there, her children know the Garden.

"Mommy, where are the ducks?" one of the boys asks.

As if they have been right there, as if it were the pages of a story all along.

When she hears about this moment, Nancy knows:

It is the seed of an idea.

It is time for her to get to work.

Looking at Bob's drawings, Nancy chooses the eight poses of ducklings she likes best.

She studies them as if she were still the girl in the library, still the girl bending wire into wreaths.

Which means Nancy has to think with her hands.

She buys a duck's foot from
the butcher to study the way
its joints move.

She borrows a stuffed duck
from the library.

She feeds ducks at the pond and tries to get close enough to study the inside of their mouths.

And she thinks, not only about the size and shape and scale of ducks, but of children as well.

Wire is used to make the shape of
a thing. You can see what is there,
but what is not there, too—an
evergreen bough, a feathered wing.
You bend it, and you can imagine.

Nancy sketches;

she sculpts.

Wax, then wire,

then clay.

The building up and the taking away.

Every day, she works to get the
tip of a beak just right,

to perfect tiny tails
and little wings.

And every day, she worries. This is Bob's
book, but she does not know Bob. This
is meant for the children of Boston, but
she's not in charge of the city. Will all the
right people say yes? Because Nancy
has heard an awful lot of *no*.

In a stroke of luck, a friend knows Bob and reaches him on his little island in Maine. He agrees to come down to Boston to see Nancy's work.

When they enter Nancy's home, Bob's wife gently touches the top of Mrs. Mallard's head.

"Oh, they're wonderful!" she exclaims.

Bob, however, says nothing.

Always an artist, he observes first.

Then he asks questions about size. In his book, the ducks are mere inches. Nancy, however, is building for the outdoors.

They agree that Nancy will build examples,
Mrs. Mallard and three ducklings, in a size to fit
the Public Garden, and plan to meet again in a
few weeks. It isn't a *yes*, but it isn't a *no*.

Bob and his wife return on a cold day, snow on the ground. The ducklings sit in Nancy's studio. They are rough, unfinished. They show the tip of a head and the waddle in a walk—but are they good enough?

Finally, Bob speaks. "They might be too large," he says.

Nancy knows that sculpture always looks smaller outdoors, where the ducks are meant to live. She and a friend roll Mrs. Mallard outside and line three ducklings up behind her.

And as Bob stands, quietly observing, three
children run—quack, quack, quacking—to
come and pat the ducks.

Bob looks at Nancy.

And she knows she has her *yes*.

Out of an egg comes a duckling.

On the blank page, a line is put down, right and true, and a drawing comes to life.

Clay is shaped, and molded, and cast in bronze.

And in the garden, in Boston, the ducks are always there, always walking to their pond, where night will always fall, and they will swim to their little island and go to sleep.

Author's Note

Robert "Bob" McCloskey was born in Hamilton, Ohio, in 1914. His *Make Way for Ducklings* was published to great critical acclaim, winning the Caldecott Medal in 1942. It has remained in print ever since, selling over two million copies.

Robert McCloskey

Nancy Schön (pronounced "Shern") was born in Newton, Massachusetts, in 1928. A sculptor since childhood, her best-known work shows Mrs. Mallard and her ducklings—Jack, Kack, Lack, Mack, Nack, Ouack, Pack, and Quack—on their way to meet Mr. Mallard, just as they are in McCloskey's book. The bronze figures were installed in the Boston Public Garden on a rainy October day in 1987, perfect weather for ducks.

Nancy Schön with a wax maquette

Schön's work on the project cemented a friendship with McCloskey that lasted until his death in 2003. With his blessing, Schön went on to sculpt characters from his other books, including the boy and dog from *Lentil* and the bear from *Blueberries for Sal*.

Since their 1987 dedication, the ducklings have gone on some adventures. Jack, Ouack, and Quack have all been stolen at different points in time, setting off citywide searches by Bostonians who love their ducks. But Boston is not the only city with a *Make Way for Ducklings* statue. After First Ladies Barbara Bush and Raisa Gorbachev visited the Boston sculpture together in 1990, a replica was made and installed in Moscow's Novodevichy Park, a gesture of peace and goodwill from the children of the United States to the children of the USSR.

Ducklings dressed for pride in the Boston Public Garden

It has also become a Boston tradition to dress up Mrs. Mallard and her ducklings. They've worn everything from sports jerseys celebrating local Patriots and Red Sox teams to "Pilgrim"-style collars and hats, and even masks during the COVID-19 pandemic. Some outfits have been political statements, too: the statues have been dressed in pink hats, Black Lives Matter T-shirts, "Vote" sweaters on Election Day, and rainbow colors to celebrate Pride. One artist, Karen Alzayer, even placed metal cages over Mrs. Mallard and her ducklings in the middle of the night to protest family separations at the U.S.-Mexico border. Schön called the metal cages "brilliant," stating that the ducks, like immigrant families, were "looking for a home."

More than thirty years after the installation of the statue, and more than eighty years after the publication of McCloskey's book, Mrs. Mallard and her ducklings continue to delight and inspire us all.

Timeline

1837	The Boston Public Garden is established. It is the first public botanical garden in the United States.
1914	Bob, or John Robert McCloskey, is born in Hamilton, Ohio.
1928	Nancy Quint (later Schön) is born in Newton, Massachusetts.
1929	The Great Depression begins, leading to mass unemployment, poverty, and homelessness.
1932–1935	Bob attends Vesper George School of Art in Boston.
1933	Molly and Wally, two ducks living along the Charles River, are featured in the *Boston Globe* when they add nine ducklings to their family.
1935	Bob meets with Viking editor May Massee, who advises him to learn how to draw.
1939	World War II begins in Europe. A *LIFE* photo shoot of Bob in his apartment with live duck models is pulled from the magazine to cover Germany's invasion of Poland.
1940	Bob marries Margaret "Peggy" Durand.
1941	*Make Way for Ducklings* is published. Pearl Harbor is bombed on December 7. The United States enters World War II.
1942	Bob wins the Caldecott Medal for *Make Way for Ducklings*.
1948–1952	Nancy attends the School of the Museum of Fine Arts in Boston.
1952	Nancy marries Donald Schön and graduates from the Museum School.
1958	Bob wins a second Caldecott Medal for *Time of Wonder*.
1985	Suzanne de Monchaux proposes the sculpture in the Public Garden to Boston's mayor, Raymond Flynn. In December, Nancy begins working on prototypes.
1987	The statues are dedicated on October 4. It also marks the 150th anniversary of the Public Garden.
1990	First Ladies Barbara Bush and Raisa Gorbachev visit the sculpture in Boston, greeted by students from the Mather School.
1991	Copies of the ducklings are installed in Moscow's Novodevichy Park. The dedication is included as part of the ceremonies surrounding the START Treaty, an effort between the United States and the USSR to reduce nuclear arms. Both Bob and Nancy are in attendance.
2003	*Make Way for Ducklings* is named the official children's book of the Commonwealth of Massachusetts. A third-grade class from Canton, Massachusetts, sponsors the legislation. Robert McCloskey dies at age 88 in Deer Isle, Maine.

Selected Bibliography

Miller, Bertha E., and Elinor Whitney Field. *Caldecott Medal Books: 1938–1957*. Boston: Horn Book, 1966.

Schindel, Morton, director. *Robert McCloskey*. Weston Woods Studios, 1965.

Schmidt, Gary D. *Robert McCloskey*. Boston: Twayne, 1990.

Schön, Nancy. *Make Way for Nancy: A Life in Public Art*. Boston: David R. Godine, 2017.

Schön, Nancy. Personal interview. May 23, 2020.

Smith, Rosalind. "Ducklings Join the Swanboats," *The Boston Globe,* May 3, 1987.